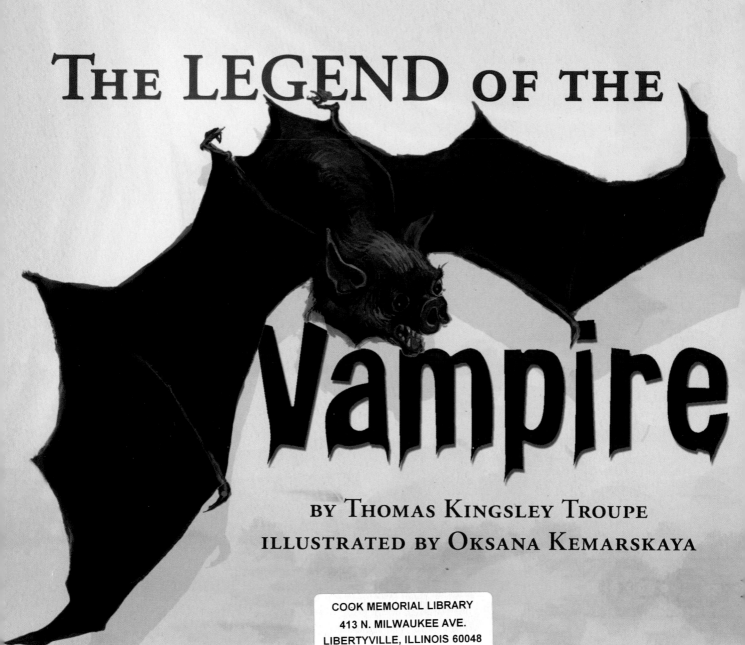

THE LEGEND OF THE

Vampire

BY THOMAS KINGSLEY TROUPE

ILLUSTRATED BY OKSANA KEMARSKAYA

PICTURE WINDOW BOOKS
a capstone imprint

Thanks to our advisers for their expertise, research, and advice:

Elizabeth Tucker, Professor of English
Binghamton University
Binghamton, New York

Terry Flaherty, PhD, Professor of English
Minnesota State University, Mankato

Editor: Jennifer Besel
Designer: Nathan Gassman
Production Specialist: Jane Klenk
The illustrations in this book were created digitally.

Picture Window Books
151 Good Counsel Drive
P.O. Box 669
Mankato, MN 56002-0669
877-845-8392
www.capstonepub.com

Printed in the United States of America in North Mankato, Minnesota.
032010
005740CGF10

All books published by Picture Window Books
are manufactured with paper containing at least
10 percent post-consumer waste.

Library of Congress Cataloging-in-Publication Data
Troupe, Thomas Kingsley.
The legend of the vampire / by Thomas Kingsley Troupe ; illustrated
by Oksana Kemarskaya.
p. cm.—(Legend has it)
Includes bibliographical references and index.
Summary: "Describes the legends of vampires, including how they started and what the
legend says about the monster"—Provided by publisher.
ISBN 978-1-4048-6031-5 (lib. bdg.)
1. Vampires—Juvenile literature. I. Title. II. Series.
BF1556.T76 2011
398.45—dc22   2009050170

TABLE of CONTENTS

The VAMPIRE AWAKENS

The sun has set. A vampire rises from its sleep. With sharp fangs, it waits to strike.

The vampire is thirsty for blood!

Vampire stories started long ago in eastern Europe. Tales told of dead people who wake to drink blood.

Vampire legends may have started because of a real person. In the 1400s, **Vlad Dracula** ruled Wallachia. Today this area is part of Romania.

Vlad was a mean ruler. He drove stakes into his enemies. He may even have licked their blood. Stories about Vlad traveled across Europe.

Stories of bloodsucking creatures

soon spread through Europe. People grew scared that bodies would crawl out of graves.

To keep vampires in their coffins, people in Transylvania built coffins with silver nails. They believed vampires were afraid of silver.

Some people even believed their living friends were vampires!

BECOMING A VAMPIRE

Stories say a vampire smells blood from a long distance—even through a person's skin. The vampire bites a person in the neck and sucks out the warm blood. The victim then becomes a vampire.

In stories, vampires look mostly like humans.
But they have **pale skin** and **dark eyes**.

Sharp fangs stick out when
these monsters are hungry.

Their fingernails grow long and thick.

Stories say that vampires have cold skin. A living person's skin feels warm. A vampire feels as cold as a glass of milk.

You won't see a vampire in a mirror. Vampires do not have reflections. These monsters do not make shadows either.

They are very sneaky.

Many stories say vampires can change into mist or bats. As mist, they slip into small places. When turned into bats, they fly to find victims.

Vampires cannot enter a home unless
invited in. But who would let a vampire
inside their house?

FIGHTING a VAMPIRE

Vampires sleep in coffins during the day. They burst into flame if caught in sunlight.

Tricking

a vampire into
sunlight is a good
way to kill it.

Vampires hide their coffins in caves or castle dungeons. They need to stay hidden from vampire hunters. Hunters try to catch the monsters in coffins. It's much easier to kill a sleeping vampire!

Vampire hunters carry wooden stakes.
Stories say that a wooden stake through
the heart is another way to kill a vampire.

Vampires hate the smell of garlic. Wearing a necklace of garlic keeps vampires away. Garlic hung on a door is another way to keep vampires from entering a house.

VAMPIRES of the WORLD

Other parts of the world have different vampire legends. In China, people kept cats from jumping over bodies. They thought cats left evil in the body. The body would then turn into a vampire.

In Greece, vampires were called vrykolakas (vree-KO-la-kahss). Stories said lightning or fire could kill these wolflike vampires.

VRYKOLAKAS

In Africa, tales tell of the ramanga. This living vampire is said to drink blood. It also eats nail clippings.

Yuck!

Legends of vampires can be frightening. These monsters aren't real. But keep some garlic handy, just in case!

GLOSSARY

coffin—a long container into which a dead body is placed

fang—a sharp, pointed tooth

legend—a story handed down from earlier times that could seem believable

reflection—an image of something on a shiny surface

stake—a thick, pointy stick; stake can also mean to stab

victim—a person who is hurt, killed, or made to suffer

READ MORE

Besel, Jennifer M. *Vampires*. Monsters. Mankato, Minn.: Capstone Press, 2007.

McMeans, Bonnie. *Vampires*. Mysterious Encounters. San Diego: KidHaven Press, 2006.

Pipe, Jim. *Vampires*. Tales of Horror. New York: Bearport Pub., 2007.

INTERNET SITES

FactHound offers a safe, fun way to find Internet sites related to this book. All of the sites on FactHound have been researched by our staff.

Here's all you do:

Visit *www.facthound.com*

FactHound will fetch the best sites for you!

INDEX

LEGEND HAS IT
OTHER TITLES

The Legend of the Bermuda Triangle

The Legend of Bigfoot

The Legend of the Werewolf

32